SHIMMER
& OTHER TEXTS

SHIMMER
& OTHER TEXTS

JOHN
O'KEEFE

THEATRE COMMUNICATIONS GROUP
1989

Published by Theatre Communications Group, Inc., 355 Lexington Ave., New York, NY 10017.

TCG gratefully acknowledges public funds from the National Endowment for the Arts, the New York State Council on the Arts and the New York City Department of Cultural Affairs, in addition to the generous support of the following foundations and corporations: Alcoa Foundation; Ameritech Foundation; ARCO Foundation; AT&T Foundation; Beatrice Foundation; Center for Arts Criticism; Citicorp/Citibank; Common Wealth Fund; Consolidated Edison Company of New York; Eleanor Naylor Dana Charitable Trust; Dayton Hudson Foundation; Exxon Corporation; Ford Foundation; Japan-United States Friendship Commission; Jerome Foundation; Andrew W. Mellon Foundation; Mobil Foundation; National Broadcasting Company; New York Community Trust; New York Times Company Foundation; Pew Charitable Trusts; Philip Morris Companies; Rockefeller Foundation; Scherman Foundation; Shell Oil Company Foundation; Shubert Foundation; Lila Wallace-Reader's Digest Fund; Xerox Foundation.

Book design by G&H SOHO Ltd.

Cover photograph copyright © 1989 by Tom Brasil.

Library of Congress Cataloging-in-Publication Data

O'Keefe, John, 1940–
    Shimmer & other texts / John O'Keefe.
    ISBN 1-55936-002-X
    I. Title. II. Title: Shimmer and other texts.
PS3565.K39S55   1989
812'.54–dc20   89-20312
                                        CIP

First Edition, November 1989

CONTENTS

SHIMMER

Originally produced by the American Inroad Series at Life on the Water in San Francisco, Shimmer *was first performed by the author on January 5, 1988. Since then O'Keefe has taken the piece to Los Angeles, Hartford, Philadelphia and New York. Among the awards he has won for* Shimmer *are the 1988 Drama Critics Circle Award for Solo Performance in San Francisco and a 1989 New York Dance and Performance Choreographer/Creator Award.*

———————————

This story is true. Most of it. It was the end of a long bad time. The fall of 1956. In the heartland of America, Tama County Juvenile Home in Tama/Toledo Iowa, just off Highway 30. It was a home for kids from broken families. Most of us hadn't broken the law. Me, I didn't even swear.

Had this tall red brick chimney that stuck up out of it. I can remember others, seven, eight, nine tall red brick chimneys sticking out of the flat midwestern landscape, Nebraska, Iowa, Illinois. God and razor straps. Five long razor straps in Tama/Toledo, lined up and hanging on the wall, with holes in the top so that they'd whistle and make tattoos, hanging right where you could see them. Tama/Toledo, the worst and the best, best because it was the last, worst because the razor straps were harder to take the older you got, best because I met Gary Welch and we discovered Shimmer.

Gary was shorter than me. Had sandy-colored hair and a big honker of a nose that hooked out so that you could see up it. I'm glad he didn't have much nose hair because I spent a lot of time with him. Came from Des Moines. The biggest city in the state. Gary was a year younger than me. I was almost sixteen.

I met him during a fight. Kept sticking his chin out at Dewey Wheeler and getting it popped. Dewey had these big sharp knuckles you could cut grass with. But Gary kept on coming at him. Dewey could have totally dismantled him if Teats Brewer hadn't stepped in and stopped it all. Teats was a big black kid, called them Negroes in '56. He was called Teats because he had the biggest set of pecs in the home. A light-skinned black guy with the fastest hands I've ever seen.

Teats started pushing Dewey back, calling him trash-face and mongo-boy, short for Mongoloid (Dewey wasn't that smart). Dewey backed off waving his hand like he was trying to say good-bye to a girl that didn't like him. And ole Teats he was strutting and talking like Amos and Andy, flapping his hands around like he was sending signals to a ship out at sea. He'd made his point; he was king of the field, except for Richard Mathison. But Richard Mathison wasn't on the playing field. He was in Lockup and he had two weeks to go, so Teats, he was having a heyday.

After everybody cleared off I saw Gary sitting on the grass trying to keep the blood off his duds. Ole Mr. White see them dirty and he'd kick him in the shins. Good ole Mr. White, patron of Hoover Hall. That was our cottage. Fast with his hands. Almost as fast as Teats Brewer except he didn't pull his punches. Five foot six, mean as mosquito meat. Talk to you one moment, nodding and bobbing his head full of good cheer and confidentiality, next moment on you like a thin cloud of bad gas, hands and feet flying, every one of them too, every one of them reaching their mark and their mark was you, sucker. Went off on Teats a lot. Made him mad as hell the way Teats could cover himself. Tried to pull ole Teats' arms and legs away but couldn't budge them. "You chicken shit, son of a bitch, chicken shit, son of a bitch." And Teats, you could just see him beneath the blur of Whitey's flying limbs, believe it or not, giggling. Teats was an astronaut of beatings. He could enter that dimension and come back like you and me can walk through doors.

"Goddamned Teats. I had that son of a bitch."

He pulled his pants up. His cuffs were over his heels.

"I hate these motherfuckers, ole man White's wife's keeps giving me these long pants. She's trying to turn me into a duck."

"She'll get numb pretty soon."

"Numb?"

"After a while she'll forget you're here unless you remind her. Old man White's another story."

"Yeah, the story of my life."

"I'm John."

"I know, Captain Spacy."

I hated that name. I got it because I wanted to be an astronaut. It was just the beginning of the space age, remember? They were shooting guys down railroad tracks at the speed of sound and blowing up rockets on launch pads but I wanted to go up there.

"Yeah, I'm Captain Spacy."
"Space ain't so bad."
He looked up at the tall red brick chimney.
"It's gonna blow soon."
"The whistle at the physical plant?"
"Yeah."
"At five o'clock."
"Makes me nervous waiting for it."
"Yeah?"
"It's not because it's loud. It's because I know it's gonna happen."
"Yeah."
"It's neat."
"Yeah."
"I ain't crazy, you know."
"I know."

Just then the whistle at the physical plant blew. We looked at each other as the sound ripped through us, grins of pain and confirmation shifting through our faces. The kids ran toward the cottages, calling out to each other. I watched their heads bob and their hair flash in the September sun. The wind came up, could feel it whisper through my hair. I knew it was saying something. I wanted to know what it was saying.

"Race you up the hill."
"All right."
I dug my feet into the grass and pushed off into space. I left Gary behind me. I was fast in those days.

"Penguins really live in the ice. Below the water. So do seals. They dive into the water and they go down into the ice and they go far enough that they get to a place where the ice is so cold it isn't cold anymore. It gets hard instead like super concrete. And it's totally smooth."

"But isn't it dark down there?"

"No, there's light."

"Where does the light come from?"

"I don't know. It's just there."

"Right."

"It's a blue-green glow."

"Like that blue-green you see sometimes in the snow."

"Exactly, it leaks up there."

"Oh."

"Below the ice you find all these places."

"The seals go down there?"

"Yeah."

"What do they do down there?"

"They do everything that we do, but they do it before we do it. We just do it and we act like we did it first."

"You mean there are penguins and seals that look just like you and me and they're in the Home?"

"Yeah, but the Home's different there. It's neat. You get to see girls and drive around."

"Are there people who've ever gotten down there?"

"Yeah. And they tried to bring things up with them."

"What kinds of things?"

"Things they'd never seen before."

"What happened?"

"By the time they got something to the top it had turned into water."

Gary and me found times to make up stories. By the window facing the playing field where we first met, or on the playing field itself, throwing a baseball.

(Fwack) "I don't like to swear." *(Fwung)*

"You've got to swear, Spacy, *(Fwack)* if you want to talk." *(Fwung)*

"Swearing isn't a sign of good language." *(Fwack/Fwung)*

"Yes it is. Swearing's where you pour the hot iron in. *(Fwack)* Like look at those *fucking* stars."

"Throw the ball."

"Right. What is it when you say *(Fwung) darn it?*"

(Fwack) "I don't want to swear." *(Fwung)*

"Swearing's *(Fwack)* good for you. It's what you say when you mean something." *(Fwung)*

"Deep, Welch, deep." *(Fwack/Fwung)*

"It's true. Just tell it to me *(Fwack)* like you'd tell one of your priesties. What is it, 'Admit it, son, admit it.' What is it when you say *(Fwung) darn it?*"

(Fwack)

"Damn it."

(Fwung)

"Shadows in the *(Fwack)* night, buddy, shadows. What is it *(Fwung)* when you say *heck?*"

(Fwack) "Hell." *(Fwung)*

(Fwack) "What is it when you say *shoot?*" *(Fwung)*

(Fwack) "Shit." *(Fwung)*

(Fwack) "You're getting pure."

"What is it when you say *(Fwung) frig?*"

(Fwack)

"Come on."

"Come on, say it."

(Fwung)

"Fuck."

(Fwack) "What is it when you say *(Fwung) gosh darn it?*"

(Fwack) "Come on."

"Come on, say it."

(Fwung) "Fuck it."

"No, that's not it."

(Fwack) "Goddamn it." *(Fwung)*

"Right!"

Gary and me pulled cafeteria. We had to be there at 5:00 A.M., an hour before the rest of the kids got up. Most of the kids hated kitchen duty, but Gary and me, we liked it because we could walk under the Iowa sky, ablaze with its Easter-egg light, the air filled with the sound of roosters and dogs and birds, and our leather shoes as we walked from Hoover Hall to the cafeteria.

(Click-click)
"People don't think dogs can think."
"I think they do."
(Click-click)
"So do I."
(Click-click)
"I think birds can think."
"I do too."
(Click-click)
"I think bugs can think."
"So do I. I think worms can think."
"Me too."
(Click-click)
"I think dirt thinks."
"I don't know, it would be hard on the dirt, all those people walking around on it and digging into it. Anyway, what parts of dirt, the little parts or the whole ground?"
(Click-click)
"The little parts think like the little parts and the ground thinks like the little parts when it thinks of itself being the field."
(Click-click)
"Well, where does the field end?"
"Where the fences are."
"Why there?"
(Click-click)
"Because the fences tell the ground when it's a field."

The cafeteria was one of the most exciting places of all because it was where everybody came together, i.e., the boys and the girls. Everyone waited outside the cafeteria. The bell would ring and everyone would file in according to cottage. One of the patrons would begin the prayer.

"Bless us, oh Lord
for these thy gifts
which we are about to receive
from thy bounty
in the name of Jesus Christ, our Lord,
amen."

The rustle of chairs, the clinking and clanking of silverware and plates and then, silence. There was absolutely no talking allowed. The sections were patrolled by patrons and matrons who paced the aisles between the tables. Evy, big, fat-faced, black-haired grinner, would roll between the boys' tables with his arms folded over his potbelly, just waiting to give his infamous ear clap, which meant that he would attempt to clap his hands together with your head between them. He could come up on you so quiet you didn't know he was there and no matter how much winking and finger-twitching the guy on the other side of you gave he would inevitably catch you whispering to a buddy or gazing at a girl across the room, and then Pop!—a mind-blackening explosion would send your ears wailing. And ole Evy wouldn't say a word, he'd just float on down the aisle with that same grin.

Going together in the Home meant sneaking glances at each other across the cafeteria.

"Is someone looking at Beatrice? Who is looking at you? Stand up and show us who is looking at you."

She stands up. She doesn't look at him. She doesn't want to get him in trouble. The matron slaps her.

"Who is looking at you?"

She doesn't look. She slaps her.

"I said, who is looking at you?"

She slaps her again and still she doesn't look at him.

Davey stands up and looks at her. Evy strides over to him and says, "What are you looking at boy? Sit down."

Davey doesn't sit. Evy shoves him down in his chair. Davey gets up. Evy slaps him. Davey doesn't sit down. Evy whacks him across the back of the head. Davey's chin smacks against his chest.

He lifts his head up and looks across the cafeteria at Beatrice. The fat matron has stopped slapping her. Everybody in the room is looking at him except for her. Davey smiles, blood's coming from the corner of his mouth. Davey's bit his tongue pretty bad. Evy grabs Davey by the collar and pushes him out of the cafeteria. The fat-cow matron tells Beatrice to sit down and keep her eyes to herself. She does. That's love. Love in the Home.

We looked at a lot of codes, Morse code, semaphore, Braille, the Greek alphabet, sign language. We even made up our own sign language. Teats Brewer caught us signing to each other and made us teach it to him. He was real good at it. The only trouble was he laughed a lot and jumped around on his bed so that ole man White caught us and made all of us hold paper to the wall for two hours. Teats started inventing a new code with his face. Pulling both eyebrows up meant one thing, pulling them down meant another, lifting one meant something else, smiling with both corners of the mouth, smiling with the right side, closing the left eyelid, thrusting the lower jaw out, sticking the front teeth over the lower lip, pursing the lips, wrinkling the nose, crossing both eyes, crossing one eye. It's a miracle we didn't get killed out there, but ole Whitey didn't hear us laughing.

"Who's receiving the code?"
"Anybody who tunes in. They catch this wave and its talk, and they pass it on."
"And we get it?"
"Right, but we don't know we got it, we just act like nothing's happened. Like static on the radio, we think it's noise but it's really talk. We're not smart enough to get it."
"Like smoke coming off a cigarette, it's like smoke signals for really smart Indians."
"Exactly."
"Who's sending the code?"
"Everything."
"What's it being sent to?"

"To whatever's signaling."

"What is that, God?"

"Yeah, but a weird god, weirder than a jellyfish. You'd throw up if you saw it."

"What would you call this code?"

"I don't know. It's not just a code, it's a language. It's on the edge of things."

"Yeah, it shines."

"Yeah, it shimmers."

"That's it."

"What's it?"

"That's the name."

"Shimmers?"

"No, Shimmer."

"Shimmer. Yeah..."

While we were working on the basic principles of Shimmer Richard Mathison got out of Lockup.

Richard Mathison was a mongrel Hun with a bit of bad Celt mixed in. Biggest fifteen-year-old I ever saw. Wasn't quite six feet. didn't weigh more than 160, but all the same, everything about him was big. Sandy-haired, with this huge face and thick, insensitive skin and a mood that could cook and freeze a TV dinner at the same time. His hands looked like they were made out of big dicks. He made Teats look like an exotic butterfly.

And there was Mathison's sidekick, Tony Kemler. Most of the time he just moved around with a convivial grin. But when Mathison was on the prowl he turned into his straight man, a straight man from hell.

And so Mathison was among us again and Welch would have to face him. To let him pee on him, so to speak, the way dogs do.

We walked down the hill together from the dairy to the cottage.

"Is he gonna beat the shit out of me?"

"Not as long as you shut up."

"What am I supposed to shut up about?"

"Everything."

"Great. What if he asks me a question?"

"I don't know. Just don't be aggressive."

"What does that mean?"

"Don't laugh. Don't smile. Don't make your face blank. Don't look sad."

"Just look scared, right?"

"Yeah, but not timid."

"How bad is this guy?"

"He's bad."

The whistle blew.

"He looks Italian to me, Richard."

"Why's that, Tony?"

"He's got a big nose and a little dick."

"No shit?"

"But I might be wrong. I ain't never seen it swolled up. Probably when he gets a hard-on so much blood goes down there he passes out."

"Yeah, that would be something to see. Well, what will get him hard?"

"Captain Spacy."

"Captain Spacy, he couldn't get a rise out of nobody."

"He's changed since you been gone."

"Has he gotten tough?"

"He's really gotten tough."

"Could he beat me?"

"Jesus, I don't know."

"I want to know."

"I don't know."

"Don't fuck with me, Tony!"

"Yes, he could beat you."

"Goddamn that son of a bitch, where is he?"

"He's right there, in the shower, Richard."

"Are you in the shower, Space Boy? There you are. Wow, you've grown?"

"He looks tough, don't he?"

"I don't think so. He's really bony."

"You're right, he looks like he's gonna cry."

"Where's his buddy?"

"In the shower over there."

"No shit? Is he tough?"

"No, he's weird."

"Where is he? Oh, he's neat. You're right, he must be Italian."

"They hang out together."

"That's neat. Hey, Spacy, come here. You slicing the biscuit with this boy?"

"No."

"Fuck off, you fat slob."

"What'd he say, Tony?"

"Jesus Christ, I don't know."

"He say something to me, Tony?"

"I said you're a blimp, muscle-face."

"Did he call me a fucking name, Tony?"

"No, ain't no name ugly as you."

Mathison put his big hand full of dicks right into Gary's face and smashed his head against the shower stall. Gary went down. Everybody backed away. Mathison stepped into the shower stall. And I went off. That's right I went off on Richard Mathison. Admittedly, his back was to me, but I went off on him. It was all like a dream. I threw my fist (it was my right hand) into the side of his head with all my might. It was crazy, I had this loving feeling mingled with a suicidal glee and this clarity, like riding the rail to a predestined and preposterous act. His head snapped and I distinctly saw spit fly from his mouth. Boxer's spit. I had made boxer's spit fly from Richard Mathison's mouth. I wondered what would fly from mine after he got through with me. But Mathison wasn't doing anything at that moment but going down. I watched him aghast, completely jarred off. So was everybody else. They gazed at me with the disbelief and curiosity of witnesses at an execution. What I did next to Mr. White probably saved me from hospitalization. I got Lockup instead. I slugged him. That's right. His face no sooner appeared around the shower stall than I swung at it. Call it a reflex. His face was bony and hard. Mathison's was meaty and soft. I understood, for a moment, the reason why guys liked to fight each other, it's like petting, except it was hard and very fast. But Mr. White didn't go down. He grabbed the back of my head and brought my face down into his quickly rising knee. Miraculously (I had a butch) he was somehow able to grab me by the hair and throw my face into his left fist. And it was there, I think, believe it or not, I had my first Shimmer. And before we struck, that shower drain and me, I entered that place Gary was talking about, where the seals and penguins go, I Shimmered my dad.

> Mother's keeping quiet in the corner.
> She knows, she knows
> ain't no law this side of custody.
> Ain't no law. Ain't no law.

> Hear the alcohol ripping through his veins.
> "This is your dad, baby. Crossed
> the dividing line some years ago,
> just before you was born."

> "Johnny, Johnny,
> sing him to sleep.
> Sing him that song he likes.
> Goes like this:

>> *Tweedle o'twill*
>> *knocking on corn wood,*
>> *tweedle o'twill*
>> *knocking on silk."*

> "Oh, Jesus, here it comes.
> I'm gonna shout,
> Johnny,
> I'm gonna shout.

> Why are you looking at me?
> What are you looking at me for?

What are you looking at?
What do you think you see?

SMACK!

Hey, Johnny,
why ain't this going right?
Just wanted to give your mama a kiss.
I'm in trouble now, ain't I, son?"

> *Tweedle o'twill*
> *knocking on corn wood,*
> *tweedle o'twill*
> *knocking on rice.*

"Now I'm talking to *you* son,
Now I'm talking to *you*.
Can you hear me?
Can you hear me talking to *you*?

What is he doing, trying to keep me down?
Is he trying to keep me down?
Is he trying to fool me, honey?
He's singing. Why is he singing?"

SMACK!

What's that word,
they call it?
Surrender.
Yes, yes,

Surrender.
In this big, wide world
full of sin.
Surrender.

SMACK!

> My daddy goes a-hunting
> He loves those birds
> loves those bass
> Why ain't the world like that?
> Why ain't the world like that?

My daddy, got to know the other side of his angry face. SMACK! We hit, that shower drain and me.

A towel was stuffed in my bloody face and my head was directed by a sure anonymous hand (probably Mr. White's) out of the showers, up the stairs, and into a moon-filled Iowa night, over a white sidewalk and into the little two-story cottage called Lockup.

A fat-faced stupefied-looking man led me up the stairs, his big ass rocking back and forth making his keys jingle. Mr. Kibby, a Methodist from Muskatine. A door was opened, the hand on the back of my head gave me a shove. I heard the door slam and I was in darkness. I groped around, keeping a hand on the towel that was soaking up the blood coming out of my face. I found a cot and sat down. It squeaked. I hated the sound of squeaking beds. They frightened me and turned me on. They had a petty sound that told you every time you turned that you were alone and that you couldn't sleep.

> *(Squeak-squeak)*
> All the memories.
> *(Squeak-squeak)*
> The time when you came into this place.
> *(Squeak-squeak)*
> The time just before you came.
> *(Squeak-squeak)*
> A classroom.
> Ames Iowa.
> Mid-afternoon, ten of three.
> A pretty girl with blond hair smiles at me and turns her head.

I'm looking down at the cuneiform between my hands, I know it's English, but I can barely read it. Sixth grade.
> *(Squeak-squeak)*

I hear a phone ring in the hall. Somehow I know it's for me.
(Squeak-squeak)

The Principal comes in the room. My heart is pounding. He looks at me. My heart pounds harder.
(Squeak-squeak)

"Johnny, could you come with me?"
(Squeak-squeak)

The kids turn their heads and watch me. The blond girl catches my eyes and turns away.
(Squeak-squeak)

I don't want to leave. But I am already in the hall. There's a cool light on my skin, but I think, maybe I'm on fire. But I'm not. There is no glow coming from me. The Principal looks at least six feet taller than me. His face is made of white iron, his smile is soldered on. He's holding my hand as if I was a toddler, I think
(Squeak-squeak)

maybe I am.

We are moving toward his frost-glass door. I know there are people in there waiting for me. I can see their shadows tilting as if they were behind a wall of ice. The Principal is opening the door. My face is freezing and yet it is aflame. It is breaking apart.

"Hey, Johnny, we're taking you to a real neat place. You'll really like it."

I can feel their nervousness like they're ready to catch someone who is very fast.
(Squeak-squeak)

"Where's my mother?"

I don't want to say those words but they're coming out of my mouth.

"She's okay."

They have their hands on my back.
(Squeak-squeak)

They're moving me towards the door. I'm starting to cry.
(Squeak-squeak)

I can hear it. I can see it but there's no one there, just this clumsy terror turning my arms and legs into pudding. A fast-paced comedy man shifting into another world but not here, not here. . .
(Squeak-squeak)

I hear this voice coming out of me, it's at least an octave higher than the one I used to have.

"What kind of place are you talking about? Are there really great kids there?"

(Squeak-squeak)

My cheeks are sticky I don't dare wipe them because I'm cool.

"Yeah, there are."

We're walking through the parking lot. The sunlight is warm. There's no mood music playing the end of the world. The "free kids" are playing on the swings and the jungle gyms. Yes, I've already

(Squeak-squeak)

crossed over the line.

There's a car with a crest on it that says "State of Iowa Welfare Department." Welcome back, brother, it's been a little while.

(Squeak-squeak/Squeak-squeak)

I run for it. In that brief moment of freedom (about ten seconds) I watch the big elms rush toward me, and I do, for a moment, think I hear mood music, it's a love song, the big midwestern cumulus are dancing over my head. Someone's got my legs, I'm hitting the ground. I can smell the freshly mowed grass.

"Come on, son, don't be a problem."

No problem. No problem.

The bed didn't stop squeaking, but I didn't hear it, I had fallen. . .to sleep.

There was a blast of light.

Mr. Kibby comes into the room and sways toward the sink. He turns on the water faucet, he begins washing my face.

"I'm sixty-five, how old are you?"

"Be sixteen in October."

"Be good to yourself."

"Yes sir."

"You know what I mean by good?"

"No sir."

"Cherish your temple."

"Yes sir."

"You know what I mean by that, son?"

"I think so, sir."

"The Lord's watching you all the time. You want the Lord to see you doing that?"

"No sir."

"You be good, I'll let you walk around."

"Yes sir. Sir, I'm sorry for crying and I want you to know that I want to be quiet."

"You talk odd son, are you with us?"

"Yes sir."

"You scared? Just keep yourself in the Holy Hand of Jesus."

He puts his big palm on my head, the bottom of it drips down over my face.

"You shouldn't be in a place like this."

He puts the side of his lips against my left ear.

"I can tell that. You're a gentle boy."

I turned the light off and sat in the dark on the bed and tried not to let it squeak. Sometimes I wanted to get up and ram my head into the wall. Sometimes I just sat there and shook my head back and forth, whimpering until snot was flying off my lips.

(Squeak-squeak)

And Mr. Kibby's shadow would appear with his slashing box of light.

"Are you with the Lord?"

"Yes, yes, I'm with the Lord."

"Is it true? Is it true?"

"Yes, yes."

Sometimes everything was black and clear and I could look into that darkness and see myself looking back just as if I was sitting there looking at a mirror. Sometimes there was this inner flashbulb that would go off in my face when I wasn't looking. And every once in a while I'd feel this buzz that was specifically me and I could imagine feeling free even if I was at the bottom of a pit.

It was in Lockup I hatched the plan to make a break for freedom.

Ole Man Kibby never did "let me walk around." He came in twice with a water bucket and a broom. He sat on my cot and watched me scrub the place down. When I was done he gave me a bar of soap and some fresh towels and told me to take a cat bath in the sink. And he sat there on the cot and watched me do it. Finally, one day he came in and led me down to the bathroom. He stood there and watched me take a shower. When I was done he handed me my work clothes.

"Keep yourself near the Lord, next time you come here we'll get to know each other better."

♦

Mathison was gone when I got out. He went with a farmer in What Cheer. When haying came he was one of the best bailers. He could toss a bail like it was a marshmallow and he could do it all day. I think they kept Mathison in the Home rather than sending him to Eldora Training School because he was a good worker and the farmers liked him.

Everybody ignored me when I got out. Except for Teats, who popped the top of my head and said, "There's my man." Mr. White didn't say anything. His pencil-faced wife glared at me and reset her already locked jaw. As for Gary Welch, he avoided me.

I couldn't stand that one. It felt weird to get butterflies over a guy, but I did. I felt the *stab* when I approached him after supper and he moved away.

> *Tweedle o'twill*
> *knocking on corn wood,*
> *tweedle o'twill*
> *knocking on rice.*

My special secret for freedom shouted at him.

Mathison's watchdog, Tony Kemler, eyed me constantly. He looked up at me even while tying his shoe. He was the first one to have a conversation with me, if you could call it that. It was while we were polishing floors.

"Richard's mad, Spacy."

I didn't answer him.

"He says he's gonna bust you bad when he gets back."
I didn't say anything.
"What you gonna do?"
I didn't answer him.

Late September blew. Thunderstorms rolled past. The trees turned a different color. And still Gary wasn't talking to me. Finally, on a windy, brilliant day in October we pulled dairy together.

"Hey man, what's up?"
No answer, he moves away.
"Hey, fuck you Welch, I went down on account of your ass."
"I didn't ask you to."
"Yeah, but I did. Why ain't you talking to me?"
" 'Cause you're weird."
"Ain't no weirder than you."
"Besides your mother is a whore."
"Fuck you."
"Fuck you back. I taught you how to swear."
I threw the broom down and shoved him in the chest.
"But you didn't teach me how to fight."
Gary stepped back, his face ablaze.
"Your mother's a fucking whore."
"That's not true!"
I swing at him. It is like dreaming. He pulls his head back and I miss. His right hand is already coming into view. There is this "crack" like you get if you bite down on a jawbreaker too hard. My face snaps back. Blurrily, I hear his voice.
"You hit Mathison from behind."
I see his other hand coming at me and before it hits I stuff him in the chest. He falls back.
"You don't know nothing about my mother!"
I'm still stuffing him. He falls on his ass right in the cow shit.
"Son of a bitch!"
He starts to get up and I shove him down again.
"You don't know nothing about my mother, you son of a bitch!"
And I start crying.

Luckily, no one else was around. Mr. Viederhander was in the office testing the night's butterfat content.

Gary gets up and starts swinging at me, screaming,

"Stop crying, you son of a bitch!"

"Fuck you, Welch, fuck you." And I'm swinging at him and he's swinging at me, swinging and crying, both of us, swinging and crying.

I don't know if anything connected. I don't think so and it didn't matter because it felt so good and so bad to be there swinging and crying with Gary Welch. We swung so long our arms ached and we couldn't swing anymore. And we cried so long we started laughing. Both of us sat right down in the shit laughing and crying at the same time.

"Vat yew bouys tooing?"

Mr. Viederhander and twenty-three Holsteins were standing there, staring at us.

We got up and tried to dust ourselves off. All we got was shit stuck between our fingers. Mr. Viederhander's mouth kept twitching. He could barely keep a grin out of his face.

"Yew get tirty."

Gary and me, we walked down the hill together.

"Mathison said if he catches me talking to you he's gonna kill me."

"I was thinking while I was in Lockup. My mother lives in Marshalltown. That's about twenty-one miles from here. She lives at 144 South Van Buren."

"So?"

"We pull dairy on Monday and we build a room inside the bales, right next to the wall, right where we can see the main watering trough."

"Why?"

"Because that's where they all meet when they have their search parties. And that's where they all come back to when they're done."

"So?"

"On Wednesday we pull dairy again. We work until the whistle blows. When it blows we don't go back."

"Where do we go?"

"We go to the room we made. We wait for them to go out, we wait for them to come back in. They won't have found us 'cause we ain't gone anywhere. So they go back down to the cottages and we take off."

"We take off?"

"We take off."

"What if they find us in the barn?"

"That's the chance we got to take."

Gary didn't say anything. The hunting parties were scary. They were composed mostly of the older kids from Coleridge Cottage, sixteen to eighteen. They loved to mess up the shrimps of Hoover Hall. Also, getting caught meant an automatic two weeks in Lockup.

When we got back to the cottage we didn't hang out with each other. Tony Kemler kept his eye on both of us.

Sunday at breakfast Gary gave me the sign, a simple, single nod of the head which sent my heart pounding.

Gary got the dairy on Monday but I got the farm. Tuesday I got the kitchen, he got cottage cleanup. Wednesday he got dairy. I got the laundry. I asked Mrs. White if I could have dairy duty. She told me to shut up. And then the hand of heaven broke in. The phone rang. Mr. Viederhander was calling for me.

"Vee've gut extra verk. He's good vit de cows."

Mrs. White grunted, sucked her thin lower lip and ripped the dairy pass from the pad and handed it to me without looking up. It took everything I had not to skip out of her office.

Since I hadn't drawn dairy on Monday, I hadn't got a chance to build the hiding place. And worst of all Tony Kemler had pulled dairy with us.

"Spacy and the Welcher, ooh, if Richard only knew."

"I ain't talking to him, so leave me alone."

"I ain't talking to him either."

"That ain't gonna help you, either way, Captain Spacy."

"Then why don't you just leave it alone."

"I ain't doing nothing. Don't have to."

God, it was crazy, but I felt like I do when I'm in an airport, though at that point I had never been in one.

As the work progressed Gary and I shot covert glances at each other. It was obvious that we had to make the move soon. Tony was getting suspicious.

"Hey Welch, what are you doing, man? You're supposed to clean up this shit here."

"Oh yeah."

"Great, 'oh yeah.' "

"Why don't you fuck off, Kemler."

"You finish it up, I'm taking off."

Kemler started after him. I stepped in his way.

"You gonna do me, Space Man?"

"Come on man, just walk away."

"What do you mean?"

"Just walk away."

His eyes were shining.

I pushed him and ran. We were both blowing it.

I no sooner got out the door when Gary collared me and redirected me toward the hay barn. I dashed in after him.

"Come on."

He started pulling bales. I watched in disbelief. A hole was emerging. Monday when he got dairy he had made a room!

We got in and started pulling the bales over ourselves. Soon we were covered up. We sank down into the darkness.

"Shhh," Gary said, "he's coming after us."

But he didn't come. Not then.

Gary and I stayed in the shadows and didn't move.

And then it blew, the five-o'clock whistle. I felt my buttocks tighten as I stifled the impulse to get up and do what I always did, buckle down, crunch down, go down to the razor straps, to the cafeteria, to the showers, to the boys pointing at my pecker and laughing, to the dormitory and the 8:30 lights out, where there was too much time to sleep, and so much time to think.

There was a rustling inside the barn. Gary and I didn't move.
"Spacy, Welch, you in here?"
It was Tony Kemler.
My heart pounded, and yet it seemed like a silly game, all we had to do was get up and say, "Yeah, we're here."
More footsteps outside the barn. We didn't dare look.
"Where are de utter bouys?"
"They already went down."
"Okey dokey, well, you'd better not dally."
"Yes sir, be right there, just looking for my gloves."
"Okey dokey."
Mr. Viederhander's footsteps moving away.
"Spacy, Welch, you in here?"
Silence.
"If you are, let me go with you?"
Silence.
"Shit."
The sound of his footsteps leaving. The sound of his footsteps returning.
"Spacy? Welch? Fuck. Good luck."
The sound of his footsteps leaving.
The sound of his footsteps leaving.
The sound of his footsteps leaving.

"Gary?"
"What?"
"My eggs lake."
"What?"
"My eggs lake, damn it, I mean my legs ache."
"Shhhh."
"I'm hot."
"Me too."
"It's getting dark."
"Yeah, but not fast enough. Let's sleep."
"Yeah."

*Tweedle o'twill
knocking on corn wood,
tweedle o'twill
knocking on silk.*

"Gary?"
"Shhh. They're coming."
I heard them. First Mr. White's voice, then Evy's.
"Keep quiet, Jamison."
"Get in the truck, Don."
"Hi ho, hi ho, it's off to work we go." Laughter.
"Stop dicking off, Base."
"Yes sir." More laughter.
The sound of motors starting up.
"Spacy and Welcher, can you believe it?"
"The yoo-yoo team."
Laughter.
The sound of trucks moving away.
"Hi ho, hi ho, it's off to work we go."

Crickets.

Gary and me, we spent our time waiting for them to come back by doing what we like most, we talked.
"There's so much to do. Right now there are millions of people doing things. Chinamen are moving on the other side of the world. I can almost feel it, "the other side of the world," Chinamen moving scrap. Moving around, talking real fast to each other. And in the nighttime having a lot of sex."

"I ain't ever had sex."
"I had sex when I was nine."
"I haven't had sex."
"It's not so bad."

"If I could control myself I could live in India most of the times of the year."
"What would you do there?"

"I'd live cheap. I'd have my ticket back to America and enough rent to put a roof over my head in any part of the country."

"What part of the country?"

"Most likely a place near the woods. Where things are cheap. Where you could put yourself up for next-to-nothing."

"What would you do in India?"

"I'd just look at the place and write everything down."

"What's in India?"

"I don't know, it's cheap. The people are neat. They've got dots on their heads."

"Sometimes I think we're just gonna die. I just know it. And it's okay because it makes everything special. Even the universe is gonna die."

"How do you know?"

"I just know. Don't you?"

"Yeah, I think I do. I read it, 'the universe is gonna die.' "

"There won't be nuthin'."

"There won't be nuthin'?"

"There won't be nuthin' forever."

"God."

"But it's okay."

"Yeah. It makes everything Shimmer."

"God, I got to pee."

"I got to pee too."

"And I'm thirsty, man."

"What do we ought to do?"

"We ought to sneak out there take a leak and a drink."

"One by one?"

"Yeah, I'll go first."

Gary pushed the bales aside and climbed into the darkness. I felt the sudden cool night air.

"Gary?"

Crickets.

"Gary?"

Gary comes flying through.

"What's fucking wrong?"

"I just didn't hear you."

"Go ahead, take off."

"Okay."

I shot off into the night. I smelled the orchard air sweet and estranged. The watering trough was under the yard light. It seemed miles away but finally I saw the reflection of my face appear. My lips and the pool are kissing. I'm chewing at my own face and it's coming up water, the best cold drink I've ever had. I'm pissing and drinking at the same time when I think I can hear Gary whispering in the night.

"Get in here."

I glance down at my pee puddle. I kick some dirt over it and dash for the dark barn.

"I think they're coming."

Big lights are bouncing down the asphalt road.

And suddenly they're here, swarming out of the trucks, jumping up and down in the headlights, and the others, the bigger ones, are coming out s-l-o-w.

They're in the barn before we can breathe.

"Hurry up, light it before Evy gets here."

They're smoking Luckies.

"Give me a drag."

"Captain Spacy and the Welch, wimp city."

"Where do you think they are?"

"Maybe they're in here."

Laughter.

"Give me a drag."

"Light up another one."

"Maybe they're here."

"Light it up."

He starts to pull at the bales.

"Hey man, I'm sitting here."

The sound of a truck in the main yard.

"Ole man White. Put it out."

Evy's voice outside, "Bill, Don, you in there?"

"Yessir, just checking to see if they're in here."

"Yeah, I'll bet. Is Base in there with you?"

"Yessir, I'm here."

"Well, get your asses out here."

"Let's go."

Base's voice, "Man, if they were in here, I'm gonna be pissed."

"You ain't never gonna know."

Evy, outside, "What you boys been doing in there, smoking?"

"No sir."

"I can smell it on you. Get your asses on down to the cottage."

Feet, voices disappearing down the hill.

Crickets.

Gary's eyes with a plastic glow.

"They're gone."

"Yeah."

"Let's go."

Shimmer time pulling out the light. Dark night beauty with a half moon rising. The grass getting sweet and wet. Dark dairy buildings all around us, casting moon shadows like they were on the "other side." Down the dairy road, running, Gary and me, scared as shit, happy as hell. Gary's shirt flashing in the moonlight. Hearing my feet pounding the road, and my heart, pounding louder.

The fields stretched out from us like the wings of a huge butterfly. I could see Gary moving with me across the road. His pushing space pushed me, together we broke the resistant distance like communicators breaking a code.

"I think I just saw lights."

"Where?"

"Behind us."

Our feet slowly ran to a stop, like music melting off a record. There were lights coming behind us.

Truck lights.

"Gary, let's get down."

Gary stood stuck like a rabbit.

"Gary, come on."

Gary bolted.

"Gary, get back down here."

But Gary wasn't getting back down, he was climbing over a barbed-wire fence and getting stuck like a fly on some real bad-assed flypaper.

I knew the sound of that truck. It was White's '53 Chevy 3100. I jumped up and pulled Gary from the fence, knowing I was tearing skin as well as cloth. Gary let out this very unmanly screech and hit the ground with me.

"Come on, let's cut across the field."

I could hear the truck's big rubber brakes dragging it down to a stop and then the crack of one of its doors opening. I sprinted toward the windbreaker trees sticking up out of the darkness. All I could hear in my mind was "Gary, Gary, Gary, get going."

The wind blew up just as I hit the trees. There was this sizzling all around me and the feeling of hard unkept ground. The cottonwoods that guarded the farm were pulling down the wind.

"Gary?"

Iowa wind moving through the cottonwoods.

"Gary?"

A dog barking, sounded like a love song,

> "Run run run
> run away
> run run run
> away
> run away"

I ran toward the vague horizon, over an empty field. I ran through a farm, because it was in the way. I drank water from a trough. It tasted as good as cold milk. Dogs chased me. I tore my skin on barbed wire. My pants-legs were shredded. So were my sleeves.

And coming out of the horizon is this long string of bobbing lights. Highway 30 to Marshalltown.

I hear this sound behind me.

"John."

That was the first and last time he used my name.

"Gary?"

"Yo."

I fell flat on my back.

"I lost ole Whitey for you."

"Yeah, right, Welch."

We ran toward the string of moving lights.

We came to the edge of the highway and were just about to cross it when we saw it, Whitey's truck sitting on the shoulder of the road pointing at us like a big ugly nightmare.

"What are we gonna do?"

"Let's cross the highway."

"Right in the traffic?"

"Yeah, right through the traffic. He'll have to do a U-ee."

"We'll get killed."

"What's the difference?"

We shot across the highway. White revved his truck and started coming at us. We ran in front of him into the oncoming traffic. Car horns blared at us. I saw Gary silhouetted in the truck lights. A big rig's horn blasted. It sounded like the five-o'clock whistle. I saw Gary dive out of the lights and then they were coming at me and I dove. A pair of eyeballs flashed at me as I hit the wall of the ditch. I think I was what you call "knocked out."

I hear all these horns and people shouting. I push myself off the ground and look over the edge of the ditch. I see Gary grinning at me. He's pointing his finger. I follow it. I see White standing in the middle of the highway, trying to stop the cars. All around him cars are skidding and screeching and blaring their horns.

Then it's over. The oncoming traffic is gone and the cars behind him are gone. There was only us and the Chevy.

We're running in the middle of the highway. We're running and holding our thumbs out like we're hitchhiking. It's beginning to dawn on me how crazy this all is when out of the night a pair of car lights appear.

Gary's on the side of the road. He's picking up something

and he's running to me. He've giving me something. It's a big rock. He's got one too. The car approaching us is slowing down. We can hear Buddy Holly coming out of it. It's a Chevy Bel Air convertible and it's pulling to a stop.

"Where you going?"

A guy in Levi's and a motorcycle jacket, ducktail and all is looking at us. I'm gripping my rock.

"Marshalltown," I croak.

"Hop in."

He's saying "hop in." We're not hopping in, we're diving.

The guy is burning rubber and we're shooting off into space. Whitey is pulling his truck in front of us, unbelievable! The guy is swerving around him.

"Hey, you stupid mother, you crazy?"

Gary and I looked at each other, our faces flushed, our eyes bugged as we slid down into the plastic turquoise backseat.

"Fag?"

The guy held up a pack of Camels. I took one. A Zippo was bundled in the pack. Gary snapped open the lid and spoked the flint. We put our heads together over the oily flame and sucked. God, the taste of those Camels. We looked into the night, the glowing beauteous Bel Air beneath us, and it was no dream. Gary leaned over, carefully avoiding the rearview mirror, gripping his rock.

"I'll kill him if I have to, Spacy."

But we didn't have to. The guy brought us out of captivity like some kind of rock-and-roll Moses. He did in twenty minutes what would have taken us hours. The wind blew through my hair and as the lights of Marshalltown appeared I felt new life. Looking over at Gary I could tell he was feeling it too.

Then suddenly we were surrounded by lights and houses and streets. I watched for a sign. Not street signs. They weren't the right signs. And we didn't want the guy to know we didn't know our way around. And then I Shimmered it, a Mobil gas station. There was something about that logo, a red winged horse, and the way the station gleamed like a spaceport. I looked at Gary. He looked at me and nodded.

"You can drop us off here."

He didn't say anything, just jutted his chin and popped his thumb up like a World War II ace and left us in a cloud of burning rubber and screaming tires.

I looked up at the street sign. It said Center and Van Buren.

We ran to the Mobil station. Gary looked like hell. And so did I. I was covered with dirt. My pants were literally in tatters, my shirt had holes in several places. Gary's was ripped all the way down the back. We saw the gas jockey's jersey as he bent down to pick up an oil spout. We shot to the water fountain. Gary gulped the water as fast as he could. He made such loud slurping sounds he caught the attendant's attention. Gary immediately jumped in front of the water fountain so I could get a quick drink.

"Hey, man, how you doing?" he croaked with a crazy amiability. The guy looked at him with utter disbelief.

"What time is it, do you know?"

I gulped the water down, wishing it could be more solid, like bread, so I could get more of it down faster.

"Let's go, Doug."

I looked at Gary. He looked absolutely nuts, his eyes bugging, a guilty bucktoothed grin on his face.

We dashed down South Van Buren as fast as we could.

"Why did you call me Doug?"

"So he wouldn't know your name, stupid."

"Really smart, Welch. Not knowing my real name's gonna make a big difference."

"You got to be clean about everything you do, Spacy."

"Yeah, right, you look real clean."

We looked at the numbers. 1086, Christ, it was almost a mile away. As we traveled south we noticed the trees were thinning and the houses getting dumpier. It was beginning to look like the right neighborhood.

We crossed the viaduct over a sprawling train yard. The steam locomotives were chopping sound out of the air, starting fast and loud then immediately slowing, laying down power strokes, black and steamy like Iron-Age insects.

When we got to the houses again we couldn't find 144. 142 jumped to 146. So the best we could figure was that 144 was in the back of 142 which was like my mother's description.

"Mother? Mother?"

"What the fuck are you doing?"

"What do you think I'm doing, I'm calling my mother."

"Christ Almighty, man, do you have to say it like that?"

"How else should I say it?"

"I don't know, but you don't have to call her Mother. At least you could call her Mom."

"She doesn't like Mom."

We moved between the walls of 142 and 146. They were close together and it was dark.

"Mother? Mother?"

Gary snorted and shook his head in disgust.

I put my face next to a dark window.

"Mother?"

A face flew at me out of the dark.

"I'll get you your mother, you little son of a bitch!"

Gary dashed out of sight.

"Does Doris Calhoun live here?"

"I don't know who the fuck lives here but you're not gonna be alive if you don't start running."

"Sorry."

I sprinted into the darkness, tripped and sprawled onto the front lawn.

"Gary?" I called. "Gary?"

Gary's voice came from the shadows across the street.

"Here."

I ran toward him. He was waiting for me in the dark. He looked at me and shook his head.

"Space, man."

"It must be North Van Buren."

Into the night, skirting the streetlights, keeping close to the front yards. Running again, legs burning, we moved north. Over the viaduct, the trains pounding the surface. The Mobil station appeared again, only this time it seemed much brighter.

North Van Buren was on the other side of the light. It was black with trees. I stuffed my shirt in and knocked the dirt off my pants.

Gary just stood there.

"How are we gonna get across there?"

We gazed out at the Mobil station. It looked like it was under floodlights.

"The longer you look at it the worse it's gonna get. It's Shimmering. If we keep looking at it it's just gonna get brighter. We got to pop that fucker. We got to think like we're invisible."

Just at that moment a cop car rolled by. Gary looked at me and started laughing.

"At least we know they're out there."

We pulled back into the shadows. The cherry-top rolled out of sight.

"Let's go."

> Slow wind
> moving through the heat
> sweat cooling on our faces
> slowest I've ever crossed a street
> although I was running.
> Lights crashing on us
> two bugs in a kitchen
> running under a bin
> pretty windows gliding by us
> pulling us in.
> Don't catch me boy, don't catch me
> running on wooden feet.
> Don't catch me boy, don't catch me.
> Could hear the leaves blowing in the wind
> over there on North Van Buren Street.

We smashed through the light. I think I saw the silhouette of the gas jockey leaning on the door of the station gazing at us as we ran past him, our rags flying, our faces aflame. The trees of North Van Buren loomed over us like a dark continent. The streetlights were thrust up among the leaves, they left a soft filtered glow and welcome shadows. The asphalt had given way to a brick street. The houses were huddled together but there were pools of darkness in each yard. We slowed our pace and looked behind us. The glow of the Mobil station was like a faint galaxy. We began to look for numbers. Near the end of the block we finally found one, 64. I looked at Gary. His eyes were shining. He knew it too, if 144 wasn't right, we were lost. At that very moment we heard a car coming out of the darkness. We dove into a nearby yard. It was a cherry-top, Marshalltown Police Department; its antenna waved, we could faintly hear the sound of the police radio over our pounding hearts. It stayed there for quite a while and then, finally, turned left and coasted up North Van Buren.

"We can't go up there as long as it's up there."

"Let's sleep here until 4:00 A.M."

"How we gonna know when to wake up?"

"We'll just know."

Just then we heard the chiming of the Town Hall bell, two strokes.

Gary grinned and shook his head. It as like we were a part of some kind of transmission. Mind you, if we didn't wake up we'd be a cute sight, sleeping there in someone's front yard at nine in the morning, a crowd of Marshalltownians gathered about us. We laid down on the grass.

The grass crackled in my ear. A car rolled past us: I didn't bother to look. We were past running. If they caught us, they caught us. The sound of the car faded and I realized again that crickets were singing. I felt my eyelids slowly close.

When I opened my eyes again I found they were already open. I was sitting up. An old rag was lying on the ground next to me. I touched it and it began to wriggle. Gary's face rolled out of it. Its eyes opened and I saw Gary look out from them. There was a part of him that didn't look quite human, something in his eyes; I realized everybody was that way.

"Spaceman, let's go."

I felt him pulling on my arm.

"Spaceman, wake up."

I shook my head and the thing that was gripping my mind let go.

"It can't be more than a block away."

"Yeah."

Just then: Bong. Bong. Bong. Bong.

We dashed into the next block. There was something clear and directed about everything we did. The house had to be wood and yellow. There had to be a set of stairs going up the back. There had to be a front porch and the number 144.

122
124
130

"Gary?"

I stopped and ducked into the shadows.

"Let's cut through here."

"Why here?"

"I just have a feeling."

"Oh brother."

We ran through the backyard, kids' swings. And appearing to our right, in the next yard was a yellow house made of wood with a set of stairs running up the back. I looked at Gary. His mouth was tight, his eyes darted toward the front of the house.

"Let's check the number."

But I didn't check the number. I ran up the back stairs, knocked on the door and whispered,

"Mother?"

Gary ran into the dark.

There was no answer, so I knocked louder.

"Mother?"

I was just about to knock again when I heard footsteps behind the door.

"Who is it?"

"Mother, it's me, John."

A light snapped on behind the door. A shadow bobbed behind the dish towel being used as a curtain. The door opened.

Things happen. That anything happens at all is a miracle, or maybe it isn't. But what happened that night changed my life. My mother was on the other side of that door. And she took us in. And for the first time in my life I had breakfast at 4:00 A.M. We watched dawn come up. We heard the birds sing. After a while we heard babies crying. We smelled coffee brewing. We grinned at each other as we drank our own. All around us, on all sides was the free world. The air smelled different. The sounds sounded different. There were so many different kinds of sounds and smells. Cars started to move below. All kinds of cars. People were coming out of their houses and getting into them. As if it was just another day. But it wasn't. I could feel the world stretch out around me, could feel it bend in the horizon. Gary felt it too. We didn't need to talk, we were Shimmering.

DON'T YOU EVER CALL ME ANYTHING BUT MOTHER

Don't You Ever Call Me Anything But Mother *was first presented at the Padua Hills Playwrights Festival in Claremont, California on July 15, 1983. Tina Preston played Doris, under the author's direction. The play was later performed at Factory Place Theater and the Museum of Contemporary Art in Los Angeles, and at the Blake Street Hawkeyes Theater in Berkeley.*

———————

Doris speaks in the darkness.

John E, you should get yourself together for school. I'm not kidding, honey, you're going to be late. Just you wait and see, you'll meet all of those rough boys who hang around the streets until the last minute. Late, John E. That's when it gets dangerous. That's when the perverts come out.

The lights slowly begin to rise. They continue to rise as she speaks. She is unseen, stage right in the bedroom.

The earlier you get to school the better the crowd.

She passes from the bedroom into the kitchen. We see just a flicker of her as she crosses through the hallway.

You ought to see these clothes, they look so white. It's Cheer, that's what it is, cold-water Cheer. I always wash your clothes in cold-water Cheer. It makes them smell just like they came out of the fresh air. And the air, you know, is good for you.

Dirty clothes fly out into the hall.

These things, though, these things have got to be cleaned. I don't know where they come from. Just when I think I've got them all, up pop these...these things, just like they came up out of some sewage pipe. Well, I've got today's anyway.

More clothes fly out.

Oh, look at this. This looks terrible. Oh my!

Movie magazines fly out.

I don't know where people get such filth. You should see them. Why look at this.

An old pot flies out along with a few very old, dirty utensils.

Oh well, we can probably use them. Can't get crazy about such things. Got good hot water and soap. The soap's Ivory, John E. And that's why your mother's hands are so white and beautiful.

Suddenly she runs from the kitchen to the bedroom. Just a glimpse of her is seen.

Oh, is that the telephone? *(Unseen, into the telephone)* Hello? Hello? Oh darn it! Why didn't you tell me the telephone was ringing? You know I don't hear that well all the time. Sometimes my mind is on other things. That's your job, you know. To take care of your mother. Oh, well, it's probably just more of those bill collectors after your father. Oh, I'm so tired. I could just lie down and sleep the whole day away. John E, why don't you make this bed. I can't always be responsible for it. Make it nice, so it's soft and comfy. You know, these sheets smell so good, just like the air. And the air's clean, you know. All of the dust, all of the dust around you fell out of the air, right out of the sky, John E, and you know, that's wonderful because that's how the air gets clean. It just drops the dust right out of the sky, just like a cat, John E, just like a cat. *(The bed is finished)* Now I'm going to open the window and let the air in and the sun. The sun, John E, you should be getting it. The sun is good for you. It makes you shine. You haven't been getting enough of it either. You should be out playing ball against the house.

(Straining to get the window open, still unseen) Oh, this window won't budge. Can you imagine that? It won't budge. *(Still straining)* Oh, John E, you've just got to help me. I get so mad at this window I could break it. *(Almost weeping)* We need some air in this room. We need some air in here. Oh God, John E don't let me get all worked up. I don't want to have a blackout. Oh well, there's just nothing to be done in here. Aren't you glad you have a mother who takes care of the housecleaning? You know, there are some mothers who just lie around and look at movie magazines. That's something that I don't do. I don't let my son do it either. You're not that kind of boy are you? You don't like that stuff do you? It has nothing to do with real life, you know. It doesn't. It comes from

the Catholics, however. Well, I don't think that this is going to do at all. The lamp is on the floor. Did you do that? Oh, it's just awful here. It stinks like vomit. Excuse my language, but it does. It stinks just like vomit. Have you been throwing up in here? Well, you should clean up after yourself if you are. This is terrible, just terrible. What are these? Are these your underwear? Well, you certainly don't clean up after yourself. You should wipe yourself after going number two. There should be no stains at all in your underwear after you go "go-go." You should toss them into the clothes hamper as soon as there are any stains at all. I'll wash them in bleach and they'll be spanking clean.

The underwear is tossed into the hall.

Now, John E, your mother is done. Do you have any coffee for me? Watch out for it now, don't want to burn yourself with it. Here I come, honey.

She crosses to the door. Her hand is just visible from the hall.

Oh look, there's Faith at the window!

She goes into the kitchen. Again we just see a flash of her as she crosses between the doors. She is delighted to see the cat.

Come on, let me let you in. That's my kitty. Just hold on. Oh, John E, come here! You should just see her, she's just beautiful. Oh, isn't that cute, she's scratching at my finger through the glass.

(Suddenly very angry that John E isn't coming) John E, get in here! *(Struggling with the window)* Oh, I can't get this one open either. *(Becoming frantic)* Oh, I just can't get this window open! I'm going to break it, that's what I'm going to do! I'm going to break it! Then I suppose I'll get evicted. They'll send that house manager up here again. And I can never get him when I need something. *(Screaming)* Especially when I can't open the windows! *(Starts to cry)* Look at the kitty, I can't even touch her. *(To the cat, still crying)* Oh, go away then, go away, I can't pet you. Shoo. *(Whining)* She won't go away. She thinks she can get in. But she can't, John E, she can't. You come in here and help me. *(Silence. Then, recovered, wiping her tears)* There she goes. There she goes. Oh, just look at her jump.

Good-bye...good-bye. You know, John E, I think I'm going to be better now. I haven't been having those blackouts so often. They're just terrible. I hope you don't ever have to have them, though it passes through the family, you know. Your uncle Chuck, he has them and he's a landscaper, gets plenty of fresh air and exercise and that wife of his, even if she is a fish-eating pagan, she fixes him good, hearty food.

We hear her light a cigarette. The smoke drifts out through the doorway.

You know, John E, it's not enough to believe in God, you've got to stay in love with him.

We see her hand holding the cigarette in the hallway.

I'm still in love with Red. Do you remember when he brought that salmon back from the greenhouse? Those Norwegians, Red Ericson. Belonged to the Masons. Do you know what that means, John E, to belong to the Masons? When you get old enough you're going to join the DeMolays. Get one nod from the Masons and you're in. It's the Masons helped me get you out of that orphanage in Lincoln. I sued the whole goddamned Catholic charities. And I beat them. I got you back. And the lawyer was a Mason. Yes, John E, your mother knows a lot of powerful people.

She smokes and weeps quietly, still just out of sight.

Why do the good ones die, John E? Why didn't your father die instead of Red? God knows, he deserves to, drinking the way he does and beating me up. Yes, John E, he beat me up. He beat me up at least once a week. I had black-and-blue marks all over my body.

She has a coughing fit. She opens the refrigerator door. The refrigerator light spills into the hallway. She opens a can of beer and pours it in a glass, unseen.

You know, I'm going to have to calm myself down.

Doris enters. She is dressed in a faded yellow-and-blue terry-cloth bathrobe. She wears a pink shower cap. She has fluffy white slippers on and they are not so fluffy and not so white.

She is a woman in her mid-to-late sixties. She is very thin.
Her face is freckled and wrinkled and bony. She has no teeth.
Her lower jaw juts out and her mouth looks like a little
shrunken trunk. She has a can of beer in one hand and a glass
in the other. A cigarette sticks out of her mouth like a nail.

Where did I put my cigarettes, John E? You know I'm always
misplacing them. Sign of genius, you know. I always was smart
in school. Your uncle and me, we were the only ones to graduate
out of nine children. And Chuck, John E, he went to junior college, became a landscaper. Now that's what you're going to do,
you're going to go to college. You like plants and all that stuff. I've
seen you with plants. They like you too. And you know your direc-
tions in the woods. You could become a forest ranger, did you know
that? That would be very good for you. You could earn a lot of
money and then you could take care of your mother like you
should.

She finds the pack of Pall Malls under some newspapers.

Here they are.

She clears a place for herself in the chair, throwing rags and
skirts and papers on the floor. Her movements are not stiff.
There is a certain grace and agility and then sometimes there
is a sudden frailty and stooping and totteriness. The tottery
side takes over as she sits herself down.

I wonder what is going to be on television today? I don't know if
I'm going to watch those soap operas. They make me feel so stupid
afterwards, like I was watching people go to the bathroom. Maybe
"Perry Mason." He'll be on at three. But that music they play with
it, at the beginning and at the end, it makes me feel so
lonely-sweet.

She blows through her lips as if expelling some nasty
substance. Smoke flies out.

I don't know about "Gilligan's Island," either. I like that little boy
but the people he's with, that rich dope and his floozy wife, they
aren't Masons, that's for sure. I like the skipper though. And the

scientist, he's cute, and those girls, I think they are kind of pretty. *(She giggles)* But you shouldn't hear your mother say things like that. *(Suddenly stern, her eyes glowing with threat)* You should take care of yourself that way. Keep your hands out of your pockets.

She broods and drinks.

You're not doing any of that stuff are you? I don't want to hear about you doing any of that...that doctor stuff. You keep that thing where it's supposed to be.

She downs the rest of the beer in her glass and is immediately up on her feet walking toward the kitchen. She speaks with her back to us as she crosses up.

Do you hear what I'm saying? I'm not going to have any of that kind of stuff in my apartment.

She disappears into the kitchen. She opens the refrigerator, pops another beer, pours it into her glass. She reappears, shuffling along.

Where are you, anyway? I hope you're not doing that hiding bullshit again. Why don't you do your schoolwork? You're not getting very good grades in school, you know.

She drinks and crosses to the chair. Sits.

Lord knows, you're still shitting in your pants. Why don't you go fall asleep in a movie? Don't you know better than that at your age? Falling asleep in a movie. I just met that man. I told him how wonderful my little boy was. And then to see you screaming and hollering and pounding on the lobby door. "Mommie, Mommie, I be scared of the dark. Get me out of here." Snot coming out of your nose. Your big, fat egg-face, "Waa, waa!" Do you know what that made me look like? It made me look like a bad mother. That man never talked to me again. I take care of you. I take care of you good. You get a lot of love in this house, a lot more than we got...*(Shouting at the hallway)* And there were nine of us!

She turns back. Speaks through pained eyes.

You stinking, snot-nosed little brat. Do you know what E-X-I-T spells? Exit! To go out. Why didn't you just get up and go out, instead of shitting in your pants and bawling? *(Starts to cry)* I'm sorry, John E, I'm sorry. They're right, I'm not a good mother. I know I shouldn't have left you in the movie so long, but I get lonely, John E, I get so lonely. Sometimes I have to have company.

She stops crying, looks out between her fingers, totally changed.

(Suddenly angry, growling) Where are you? I said, where are you?

She raises her head up strangely, like a short-necked giraffe. She looks around the room.

Have you gone to school already? Have you left me here to talk to myself? You know that's not fair. It's scary to be left here all alone with myself. *(Suddenly leaning forward, whispering in her chair, talking to the air in front of her)* You know, John E, your father was afraid to be by himself? He said that it scared him, like being alone with a ghost. Isn't that frightening? Your father was a frightening man.

She goes to get another beer.

He was a bad drinker, that man.

Stops at the edge of the hallway and looks at the picture of a child. She talks to the picture, touching it gently.

But handsome, handsome like you, with curly hair and long, white fingers. You're going to be a piano player, that's what you've just got to be. *(She leans against the wall near the picture, gazing into the hall as she speaks)* But you're not going to be the kind of man your father was. You're going to be a good, gentle man and you're never going to hit women.

She drinks, then crosses into the kitchen. Speaks, unseen.

John E, do you remember that time we hitchhiked across the country? 1952. Same night that big fat slob in Moline started knocking me around. *(She cackles)* I got her back, didn't I, John E? You saw her. She was bleeding like an animal, the whore. You know what she called me? She called me a "cunt." And then do you remember what that whore said? She said that I took her old man's money.

I never called your father my "Old Man"! *(Suddenly poking her head around the door of the kitchen into the hallway, shouting)* And don't you ever call me anything but Mother!

(She fairly leaps into the hallway, shouting) Do you hear me? Don't you ever call me anything but Mother!

> *She goes back into the kitchen.*

Never, John E.

> *The can pops. She reenters the living room.*

Yes, your father was a very strong and handsome man. You know he killed his own father, don't you? Your grandfather. He kicked him right down the stairs and he kept on kicking all the way, all the way down each and every one of them. And your uncle Paul, the doctor, the one that brought you into the world? He got your father out of it. His family is very strong, not that the Calhouns aren't either, but he's got Waterloo money, *(She sits)* county coroner and hospital doctor, got them coming and going. And he's rich, filthy rich.

> *She leans over and turns on the television. It chatters in the background. She speaks about the programming.*

Oh, I don't like this stuff. It makes me feel like a housewife.

> *She flicks the set off in disgust. She crosses to the record player. She turns on a small lamp near it.*

Sometimes I don't think you can love past twenty-three, John E.

> *She puts on a record. It is country-western music. The first cut is "I'm Sending You a Big Bouquet of Roses."*

Where are my cigarettes?

> *She crosses downstage, delicate and ladylike, to her beer and pours the rest of the can into the glass. She crosses stage center beneath the overhead light and takes the end of the pull chain as if it were a precious gem, looks at it, then pulls on it. The light goes out.*

Miller's, John E, the best. That pretty girl sitting on the moon waving her leg up and down. That's me. You should know those country nights, John E.

Crosses to the kitchen, speaking as she moves.

We'll get back there again someday. There is too much light in here. Good God, you'd think there was something interesting going on out there.

She draws the kitchen window shade down and the room goes dark except for the light coming from the refrigerator as she opens it to get another beer. She pours herself a can by refrigerator light. She closes the door and crosses through the hall into the bedroom.

Oh look at this place, John E. It looks like a casket. I shouldn't see the bedroom in the daylight.

She draws the window shade down and the room goes dark. She turns on the night-light.

Oh, it looks so much better now, like the thirties. The thirties should only be seen at night, John E, at night when it's black and gold. That's when I had such red hair it'd burn your heart out. And I did, John E, I burned a lot of hearts with my hair. You can still see parts of the red in my hair. They glisten and glow. *(Suddenly enthusiastic)* Let me doll up for you, John E! Let your mother doll up for you and show you her stuff.

A light clicks on just behind the bathroom door. The record continues with "I'm Sending You a Big Bouquet of Roses."

Let me see here now. *(We hear bottles clanking as she rummages through the cabinet)* Oops.

She drops a bottle. It breaks.

I just haven't done this in such a long time I get slippery fingers. You should help me, John E, you should help me clean this up. Oh, all right, I'll just do it later. I keep this house up, don't you think? That's more than I can say for your grandmother, my mother. Did you know she couldn't even cook pancakes? Stab a fork into them and goo would run out of the center. She never made the beds. Even when your grandfather was alive. She didn't do a thing, but she always looked busy. And she didn't take care of herself either. Oh, she smelled! I mean, sometimes she smelled like she had been lying in bed with a man all of her life. You know what I mean, don't you? She smelled "that way." Stay away from women that smell "that way." They're dangerous. Oh, darn this hair. It's always had a mind of its own. But that's why it's so beautiful, John E, that's why it's like wave-water. There we are. Now just a little on my face and I'm through.

> *The record has ended and the needle swishes in eerie syncopa-tion on the tail-out groove. The bathroom door slowly opens and brilliant white light breaks from the room. Gradually the figure of Doris emerges. She is bathed in bright light. Her old face is painted with white powder. Her cheeks are covered with bright red rouge. Lipstick is smeared over her lipless, toothless mouth. Dark green eye shadow and long, false eyelashes make her look as if she has two black eyes. Her frail body is covered with a wrinkled, stained nightgown. She speaks in a soft, shy voice.*

Hello, John E, this is your mother. Do you like me? I can still draw an eye or two. Do you remember what I looked like with those shoulder pads and the Scottish plaid? I'm Irish, you know, but I look good in things like that with my hair all piled up like on a Coca-Cola sign out of the forties. I had slim legs and a lithe body and champagne breasts and my skin was creamy white with warm little freckles on it. John E, look at me. I'm going to tell you something you should know about. Look at this body. Do you know what this body is for? It is for the lust of God to have his way with me. All...the...way, John, all the way. To plant a baby inside of me. To plant a baby in me. That's where you were. You were up inside of me. *(She cups her hands between her legs)* Up here. Haven't I ever told you about that stuff? Let me tell you, my dar-ling son. A man, John E, a man put his thing in me. And it made him feel terribly good. That thing, that big thing of his. It made him want to come. Do you know what "want to come" means? It means that he can't stand the pleasure of it so much that he dies in me. He dies in me. He dies in me, John E, and when he does his whole body gets hard and starts to shudder and he starts pumping and pumping and he makes these strange cries like a baby wanting his mother and his face gets red like a poor sweet thing and he begins to weep and then, John E, then he comes. *(Mysteriously)* He comes inside of my body and I hold him and I say, "Yes, yes, my sweet darling," and I rock him and caress him and he gets all soft and cuddly and he just curls up and goes to sleep. But I don't sleep, John E, no, I don't sleep. I lie there in the dark and feel his cum go sticky, feel it up inside of me, sending its magic into me, red and wanting and hurting for the magic that will wear your eyes and dress in your skin. *(She smiles knowingly, almost winking)* Someday you'll come, John E. You'll know when you come. You'll know it for sure.

She hears the needle in the tail-out groove.

Listen to that thing. It sounds like a cat, don't you think? It sounds like a cat licking the corner of a window.

She crosses to the record player and takes the needle from the record. Her mood changes. Her voice is low and pensive.

But you didn't come out that way, John E. They had to cut you out of me like some ugly sliver. *(Calling to him)* John E! John E! I'm going to get you back. I'll get you back even if I have to come out of the ground to do it.

She stands by the record player. Her head drops. She looks around for her beer. Can't find one. Goes into the kitchen for another.

You know why your father liked me? He liked me because I could hold my beer. I could drink with the best of them, and I could, still can. I'm going to put some beans on for when you get back from school. What is this? John E, you should put the old beans back into the refrigerator. Whew, they smell awful. Why here's another pot left out. Where are all of these beans coming from?

Have you been playing around in the kitchen? *(Opens refrigerator)* Why look at this. The refrigerator is full of beans! Well, these are certainly not very fresh.

> *She crosses through the bedroom to the bathroom and dumps a pot of spoiled beans into the stool. She turns the bathroom light off, then goes back into the kitchen and dumps a big bag of beans into a tin pot.*

We'll just have to make some fresh ones. You tell me, John E, what's it all mean? Don't they teach you anything in school besides how to get bored? Have they ever told you what to do after all that get-up-and-go? I'll bet they told you all the old people go to Pasadena to the garden of Eden with Mickey Mouse. Where's my beer?

> *She reenters the living room and finds the one she left.*

I don't like the light in here.

> *She clicks the small lamp near the record player off. The living room becomes dark. She crosses back into the kitchen.*

Oh, God, I hate this light.

> *She opens the refrigerator door.*

Good God, I'm almost out of beer. Have you been getting into my beer? I told you never to get into my beer. It's my medicine, for my heart.

> *She closes the refrigerator door. The stage is in darkness.*

Oh, my God, it's so dark! I can't see. John E! I can't see!

> *She opens the refrigerator door and attempts to keep it open so that she can get to the living room by its light.*

John E, help me. Oh God, he isn't going to help me. Oh, if I can just get to the television before this door closes.

> *She enters the living room. She runs her fingers along the wall. She crosses toward the television. There is a "flunk" as the refrigerator door closes. Doris makes a frightened sound and then bashes into the table.*

Oh, no!

> *She falls to the floor and begins crawling on her hands and knees, whimpering.*

I'm having a blackout, John E! I'm having a blackout in the dark!

> *She makes a series of strange "whoops," then goes silent. She crawls to the TV in the darkness, turns it on. Her face appears, illuminated by its light.*

I think I'm going to throw up, John E! Get me a pan! Get me a pan! *(She screams at the top of her voice)* Where are you, you snot-nosed little brat!!

> *She crawls to the bathroom and throws up in the toilet. She flushes the stool. She lies down on the bathroom floor, breathing heavily.*

Oh, my heart, my heart.

> *Gradually her heavy breathing subsides. She speaks, still lying on her back.*

Get me a towel. *(Screaming)* Get me a towel! Oh, it's no use.

> *She struggles to her knees, reaches up and turns on the bathroom light. She gets a towel and wipes her face off. She drops the towel and staggers to her feet. She is dead drunk. She lurches into the living room.*

Where is my beer?

> *She searches around on the floor. She falls to one knee near where she left the can of beer.*

Here it is. You little bastard, where have you been hiding all of my beers? I'm going to have to go out and get some more.

> *She staggers to the chair, and falls to the floor next to it. The apartment is dark except for the light in the bathroom and the TV. She looks into the TV.*

Is it dark where you are now? Is it so dark you can't see your mother? Can you hear me? John E, can you hear me? *(She looks up at the light bulb)* You left me.

> *She struggles to her feet.*

You were standing over me. You had a light bulb in your hand. *(She starts to jerk the pull chain of the overhead light back and forth. The light swings wildly, going on and off)* You had a light bulb in your hand. "I'm going to smash this light bulb in your face, you dirty whore." To me. You said that to me, to your mother, John E.

> *She sinks to the floor, still holding the chain, turning the light off.*

But the worst thing is, John E, the worst thing is that you left and you didn't come back.

> *She stares at the television in silence. She dozes off. She starts.*

Is that the telephone? Is that the telephone? *(She heads for the phone)* Don't hang up, John E. Don't hang up, I'm coming. I'm coming.

> *She stops just short of the bedroom. Listens. Then falls back against the wall, knocking a small bookshelf over.*

You hung up.

> *She crawls back to the chair and climbs into it. She stares at the TV.*

I hate this garbage, "Dialing for Dollars," he ought to stick to the weather. God knows, he can't even do that very well. What a wimp. Don't you ever be a wimp, John E.

> *She looks sourly at the TV. She drinks. She sits and stares, blank-faced, then her eyelids droop.*

Going to have to get some more beer.

> *She starts to drift off.*

Wish you...could get it for me.

> *Half asleep, she speaks a combination of dream-talk and memory.*

Wish you could get me to the bus Daddy's car is on the blink used to kiss my mother so sweetly. Now he's dead. How could he kill himself, John E? He was my father. Didn't you know that I loved him?

She suddenly snaps awake.

John E, I be scared!

She realizes that she has just shouted. She looks down at the beer in her hand. She starts to lift it to her lips, pauses midway, looks out with longing, remembering.

There was...this little church we used to go to in the spring. Mother would gossip while we played in the cemetery and one day there was a rainbow. It made everything fresh and clean. I could feel my skin so young...

She stares out in silence, then reaches down and turns the TV off. She looks about the dark room. She picks up the beer and finishes it.

I know I left a half-empty around here someplace.

She starts searching the living room. She can't find it. She is on her hands and knees.

I know, I know, I left it in the bedroom.

She crawls to the bathroom. She speaks, unseen.

Yes, here it is. I'm tired already and it's not even "Perry Mason" time yet. I'm going to wake up in the middle of the night and not be able to go back to sleep. Why don't you call me then, John E? I'll be awake.

The bathroom door closes.

Good night, John E, good night.

The light in the bathroom fades to black.

THE MAN
IN THE MOON

The Man in the Moon *was first performed at the Blake Street Hawkeyes Theater in Berkeley on November 5, 1983. David Schein played The Man, under the author's direction.*

———————

It it it it
it was the moon
(I think it was the moon)
yes, it was the moon.
And and and it was shining
yes, it was shining
(It was three-quarters full)
and it was cloudy, the clouds
were rolling through very fast
and the wind was blowing and
leaves were flying and the
trees were bare and the
branches were bending
and the grass was blowing
his shape, The-Wind-Twister-Big-Steps-Magic-Man
that you couldn't see unless there was
a flag or something to blow against.
And and and it was in the sky
(I think it was in the sky)
a f...f...fish-head
cloud...un...under the moon
full of moon-smoke and submarines,
little ones following it on its flukes,
diamondbacks curling around
its snout and a big leopard
sitting on its tongue.
Gorgeous! Beautiful!
I mean it was gorgeous,
beautiful beyond belief,
this this this fish and its associates.

What are you doing,
waiting for a bus?
Dropped everything, wife, kids, car.
Got a hotel room in Iowa
stashed my clothes,
waited three days and three
nights in the nude, sweating
in the thick summer's air.
Tornado time, buckets and
jars, waiting so still.
Quiet houses and black rooms
with shades left up, white
chrysanthemums glowing
in the dark, lightning bugs
and whippoorwills, sheet lightning
plugging the black clouds
on the rim of the horizon,
and a big black dome full of shifty stars
shining through the thick lens
of air and quiet wet twilight
on the windows looking west,
(I think it was west),
dark and hot and
lonely beyond belief, the
nighthawks diving for bugs
by the streetlights, the
hard fart of a fast car heading
into the country, the beer halls
full of hot rowdy men,
each one of them mean
and hungry and tired
and sticky and lonely like me.
Three nights and three days,
you should have seen the days, they
were so heavy the flies couldn't move
and so muggy the sunlight
lost its direction, even the birds
were sweating, like hot whiskey,

impossible, just fucking impossible,
kind of made you want to die in cold stone,
Death-Wish days and darkening
thunderclouds, swamp green
and putrid, made you fear the air.
Made the houses stand on end, made
the doorways creak, made their
tongues fly out and GRAB you, and then
the rain breaking and the whole place
going up like a big plastic two-by-four,
shuddering the rain out of the sky in big
fat, hot drops. Bristle-cone lightning,
Boom-Boom-Boom (Grendel dogs chasing
their tails around in the dark with electric
matches) and the cold wind
and howling spikes of liquid ice,
climbing through the cracks in the
windows and coming down the stairs and whisking out
of the fireplaces and crumbling in
the lofts and attics,
looking out with ever-still eyes.
You know, I looked just like you once.
Put my face up, just like you, I did,
right up into the fluorescent light,
got pale as a whitefish, ate my plastic
gravy, reserved my place in the hospital,
joined Hospice, did it all
just to get where I am today.
Got the, got the bargain! Got the Eternal Life!
Got the Moon! I know the secret
and you don't. You just think you do.
But I've got to work for it.
You just do what you're told.
You all act like crazy people,
always sitting around drinking coffee
with your halters and your blinders
and your eye-masks and your soldier buttons.
But that's okay with you, right?

That's okay with you cuz nobody's going to
take my word over yours, a crazy, foulmouthed
freak like me. Nobody's ever gonna know you're a fake.
I mean, Christian God, you've worked it all out
beforehand with the Lord in Ohio three Sundays
before my mother got laid by youse all.
I'll blow you for a dollar.
I don't take quarters.
Come on, admit it,
you want to put cum all over my face.
Maybe you'd like to bash my skull in?
Maybe that's your thing. It's okay.
Maybe a little flap of skin
peeled back so you can peek in
and see what's really going on, get into
my dreams, drink all of my brain-blood
and get high?
You know how much wine I got in here?
I got nights of it.
I got days of it.
I got dirty motel rugs of it
and hot cement afternoons in the
downtown streets of it and it was nice,
nice as letting your own shit fill your
pants. I'm a junky on life!
And horse pudding and hash grease,
and Thorazine M&M's.
I've got reds, blues, and purples,
blacks and crate-yellow limes, fuck
I've sucked spit off the street
and I'm alive! Tell me, even if I
kick off this winter I'll have been
out-of-doors more than a cave man because
I've found a dream, just like
that big black demon buried in
the South, I've got it, I have.
I've got the glowing chalice-morning,

for the moon is no dead being.
She is alive and she talked to
me, still does, doing so right now.
But I didn't know it.
Went out for football instead,
got laid instead,
went to junior college instead,
inserted my life into a family instead,
held my own instead,
until I got the nod.
And it came to me just like it's
coming to you right now,
by someone who's been on the streets,
right off the streets, by this
cum-faced, jubilant hero.
Unbelievable sign, simply unbelievable!
Just like you read in books.
Here it is, right in front of
your face and you don't know
what to do about it.
Come on, come on with me.
I've got a girl for you.
She's up there right now.
You know, you've been
chasing her. You can smell
her night wind full of perfume,
her night air full
of deepest love, you know,
that green-eyed girl with
the red hair backing into
the darkness. You'll see dolphins
swimming around her face, you'll see
sea foam and turquoise and the
flush of her cheeks like some
maple leaf in Maine, lips
as red as rose hips
burning your heart out.

I'm telling you, she's up there right now
and she's got your heart and you don't
even know it. You'll see.
Next time she comes out of the
black sky in a little sliver,
you'll say, "My God, I've missed you!"
And you won't want to live
inside anymore or dress in
those silly clothes or talk to
people you think you know.
Don't you see, they're not real.
You'll be able to tell
because they'll listen
to your rap and give you that sick,
patronizing grin like what
you're saying is driving them
crazy and that's because they'll be getting
the idea that being around you
will make them disappear and they'll be right.
You know, the ones in the suits
ducking behind the Xerox machines,
sneaking, snickering, *National
Enquirer* personalities.
Jesus God, I could tank up right now,
couldn't you? Could drink myself
under until the cement got wet.
How about it? Want to tip a bottle?
You can buy it. I'll supply the labor.
Just call me your guru.
I'm the guy they mean when they tell
you to see "the great man."
Unbelievably pure, right?
Enough to make your hairs prickle.
Mine are. Can't you see that?
Mine are prickling right now.
It's the moon
It's the moon

It's me,
cuz I'm the man in the moon.
I'm the real man in the moon.
We got it on that night and we had a baby
and it was you. I know, I can tell by
your eyes. They look just like mine.
How about some brandy? You're braced.
Let's get into that luggage you're carrying
and see what's new and cool. I'll give you
something that will make your eyes melt. I know a room
where it's warm, where the nighthawks are
crying, in a town where nobody lives and where it's
all dressed up like Sunday...but the lights won't
ever come on. You can walk that town
forever and you won't see anyone. You'll hear them, but you
won't ever see them. You'll talk to them,
but there won't ever be anyone there.
You can even buy wine with the nickels
they give you and bum cigarettes from them
but they won't be able to touch you.
You can suck their cocks and shoot their
beetle-blood into your veins but they can't
touch you and that town is this town,
ain't noplace else.
It it it it's the moon and you didn't understand
but now you do. In the blue haze of dawn
while you're walking off a hangover you'll
find me under your feet looking
up at you, dead and empty as a town.
You'll know me, you'll know me like you know royalty.
So that's where I get off.
So that's where I get off.
Don't worry, you'll always be able
to find me. Cuz I'm you, that's right,
I'm you. Now you know the shotgun of the truth.
Yeah, you know. Yeah, you know. Yeah,
you know. Yeah.

I'll bet that's your bus.
Off you go into the wild blue yonder.
I won't be too far away.
We'll be sleeping in the same town.
You and me, almost side by side.
I'll be thinking about you.
I'll be thinking about you.
I will, I'll be thinking about you.